All Aboard!

A Tour of the *Holiday Train Show* at
THE NEW YORK BOTANICAL GARDEN

PHOTOGRAPHS BY ROBERT BENSON

One of the most eagerly anticipated seasonal traditions in New York, the *Holiday Train Show* has enchanted visitors to the Enid A. Haupt Conservatory since 1992. The living landscape features large-scale model trains and trolleys winding their way across trestles, over bridges, around pools, and through tunnels past scaled replicas of New York landmarks—meticulously handcrafted by Paul Busse and his team of artists at Applied Imagination from natural materials such as bark, twigs, stems, fruits, seeds, and pine cones.

Highlights among the Garden's growing collection of more than 140 iconic buildings include the Statue of Liberty, Radio City Music Hall, George Washington and Brooklyn Bridges, Ellis Island, and the original Yankee Stadium and Pennsylvania Station. With the small buildings lit from within and charming evergreens and flowering plants lit by the winter sky, the setting casts the romantic glow of old New York at twilight during the holiday season.

This tradition has been a gift to the people of New York from Founding Sponsors Victoria and Robert Zoellner and their family. On behalf of the millions of children and their parents whose spirits have been lifted by a visit to the show, we extend our heartiest thanks and appreciation.

Gregory Long

Gregory Long, *President*
The New York Botanical Garden

◀ **Little Red Lighthouse** (1880)
Below the George Washington Bridge, Manhattan
Originally located in Sandy Hook, New Jersey, the Little Red Lighthouse was moved to its present location in 1921. It was immortalized in the 1942 children's book, *The Little Red Lighthouse and the Great Gray Bridge*. After navigational lights were installed on the bridge, the lighthouse was put up for auction. The outcry from a barrage of letters from children who loved the book saved the lighthouse, and it is still maintained by the City of New York. The model, created in 2004, has siding of tinted magnolia leaves and a lotus seed pod for the peaked roof. The "light" in the windows is white birch bark.

Previous spread
The *Holiday Train Show* features some of New York City's most iconic structures such as (from left) **The Plaza Hotel**, **Saks Fifth Avenue**, the **Empire State Building**, **Metropolitan Life Insurance Company**, **Radio City Music Hall**, **Rockefeller Plaza** (**General Electric Building**, **Holiday Tree**, **Prometheus**, and **Channel Gardens**), the **Chrysler Building**, the **Flatiron Building**, the **New York Stock Exchange**, **Brooks Brothers**, and the **Brooklyn Bridge**.

Dear Friends:

It is with great pleasure that we have been associated with the *Holiday Train Show* almost from the beginning. We love the Botanical Garden and the holiday season, and are thrilled that this annual event has become such a cherished tradition for tens of thousands of New Yorkers. Bringing grandparents and grandkids, toddlers and their parents, friends and strangers together during the holiday season is a delight indeed. Everyone who comes is mesmerized by New York landmarks masterfully re-created from plant parts, by trains racing from gallery to gallery and soaring overhead, and by colorful tropical and subtropical plants all beautifully curated in one of the most spectacular settings in the world. How lucky we are to help people discover this!

May all good things be yours during this holiday season.

Victoria and Robert Zoellner

◀ The *Holiday Train Show* features landmark buildings in Manhattan and beyond such as (from left) the **Alice Austen House** on Staten Island, the **Bowne House** in Queens, and **Boscobel** in the Hudson River Valley.

To visit the *Holiday Train Show* in the Enid A. Haupt Conservatory at The New York Botanical Garden is to enter another world—a world of pure enchantment on so many levels.

Expectations are heightened by the season, which sets the stage with an undercurrent of anticipation: music, lights, parties, families reuniting, snow—or at least wintry weather—gifts, and a thousand different holiday traditions.

For the little ones, there's the thrill of seeing trains, trains, and more trains, all an understandable size, rolling along tracks in the Conservatory in a diminutive landscape that offers excitement of its own: waterfalls, tunnels, forests of glittering evergreens. Some of the train track does amazing things. It disappears around a bend and reappears high overhead crossing a bridge, only to disappear again and emerge behind a building, which magically is one's own size and made of bark, twigs, and leaves!

For those who have left behind the age of such innocent wonderment, there's the undeniable delight of seeing a meticulously created landscape within a splendid Victorian glasshouse. But that's just the beginning. Looking closer, one sees sophisticated replicas of New York buildings all made from dried plant materials: brick façades built with tiny pieces of bark, siding assembled from reeds, roofing composed of moss, 20-foot bridge spans made with branches, tunnels of hollowed logs. And then there are the details: the Statue of Liberty in a robe of palm fronds and grasses holding high a pomegranate torch with a flame of dried monarch flower, the spirals of Frank Lloyd Wright's Guggenheim Museum echoed with black locust shelf fungi in the botanical version, the marquee of Radio City Music Hall reproduced in radish and catalpa seeds.

Some of the structures are familiar landmarks, others less well known or no longer standing. Working from photographs, show creator Paul Busse and his crew create easily recognizable, small-scale translations rather than precise replicas. Just as a skilled caricaturist captures a personality with a few strokes of a pen, they capture the essential, distinguishing elements of a building with plant materials. Berries, seeds, pods, and vines add texture and detail, and, of course, are the key to making the whole design harmonious in a garden setting.

The *Holiday Train Show* combines a designer's love of trains with a landscape architect's eye for detail and an artisan's imaginative use of plants. The New York Botanical Garden and Paul began their collaboration in 1992, and every year thereafter the show has become more elaborate. It takes a crew of close to 20 about 10 days to lay out the 1,200 feet of track, construct the trestles, position the buildings, tuck in the hundreds of plants, place the lights just so, and get the

9

trains running. The track arrangement consists of simple loops, with the tracks woven into the landscape and screened by houses and plants. With as many as 14 trains and trolleys running at any time, there is always that captivating feeling of anticipation, waiting for a train to reappear.

Together with the venue of the grand Conservatory, the show makes for a delightful holiday experience. Indeed, it has become one of New York City's most beloved traditions, or as *The New York Times* puts it, "one of New York City's best holiday gifts to itself."

About the Trains

The trains in The New York Botanical Garden *Holiday Train Show* are G-gauge. Designed to run outdoors, their motors are housed in weatherproof casings. They are powered with low voltage on gauge-1 brass track, which measures 1¾ inches (45 mm) between the rails. A large-scale steam locomotive can measure over 2 feet long and weigh as much as 10 pounds.

The locomotives and railroad cars in the *Holiday Train Show* represent American trains from late 1800 steam engines to today's most modern high-speed passenger trains. Model trains, however, have existed since the inception of the railroad industry in the 1830s. Many of the earliest models were built for competitions sponsored by railroads to encourage inventors to solve early engineering problems. Others were built to gain the public's interest or to entice financial backers to support new railway lines. Afterward, these steam models—some of which were large enough to ride on—were often given to the investors' children and installed outdoors on spacious estates.

Soon toy manufacturers started making model trains. But just as in the world of full-size trains, there was no consistency in the gauge of the track or the scale of the trains. This problem was solved in the 1880s when the German company Märklin established standardized gauges and scales. Before long, almost all American and European model manufacturers had adopted these standards. Most of these railroads were still built for use outdoors and eventually the term "garden railway" came to be used to describe model railroads, which, with suitable landscaping, became decorative and entertaining features in the garden.

In 1967 the German firm of Ernst Paul Lehmann introduced Lehmann's Gross Bahn (LGB), or Lehmann's Big Trains, made of modern UV-resistant plastic and modeled on German narrow-gauge trains. They were sturdy and designed to run outdoors on standard gauge-1 track. These new LGBs were not immediately popular in the United States as there were no models of American trains. However, in 1985 LGB introduced a model of a Colorado narrow-gauge steam engine, the *Mogul*. American narrow-gauge railroads were designed as short-line systems where the terrain was too steep for standard railroads. With models of American trains now available, garden railroading as a hobby became popular in the United States. Nowadays, many U.S. manufacturers make large-scale trains—among them Aristo-Craft, Bachmann, Lionel, and USA trains.

About The New York Botanical Garden

Nathaniel Lord Britton, an eminent Columbia University botanist, and his wife, Elizabeth, also a botanist, were so inspired by their 1888 visit to the Royal Botanic Gardens, Kew, near London, they decided that New York should possess a great botanical garden. A magnificent site was selected in the northern section of the Bronx, part of which had belonged to the vast estate of tobacco merchant Pierre Lorillard. In 1891 the land was set aside by the State Legislature for the creation of "a public botanic garden of the highest class" for the City of New York. Prominent civic leaders and financiers, including Andrew Carnegie, Cornelius Vanderbilt II, and J. Pierpont Morgan, agreed to match the City's commitment to finance the buildings and improvements, initiating a public-private partnership that continues today.

Now in its second century, the Botanical Garden is one of the world's great collections of plants, the region's leading educational resource for gardening and horticulture, and an international center for plant research and conservation. The Garden is alive with opportunities for discovery, from an ecotour of the world in the Enid A. Haupt Conservatory to an innovative indoor/outdoor hands-on science museum for children, 50 exquisite gardens and plant collections, and innovative exhibitions, flower shows, and other visitor attractions—all on a 250-acre National Historic Landmark site that includes 50 acres of the old-growth Forest that once covered New York City.

In addition to the beauty of its natural topography, the scope of its plant collections, and the distinction of its designed gardens and curatorial excellence, the Botanical Garden is celebrated for the ambitious goals of its scientific research and educational programs as well as its careful stewardship of this unique site. Today the Garden is an open-air classroom, major arboretum, delightful array of display gardens, and a place of scholarship and respite.

◀ **Grand Central Terminal** (1913)
42nd Street & Park Avenue, Manhattan
This Beaux Arts-style train station embodies
the romance and glamour of the Golden Age
of Rail and remains a civic design triumph of
architecture, technology, and city planning.
The building is topped by a 1,500-ton sculpture
of Mercury, Hercules, Minerva, and an eagle,
symbolizing commerce on the move, sustained
by moral and mental energy. On the replica,
created in 1992, the rooftop sculpture is crafted
from dried strawflowers, arborvitae, and
yarrow. The façade is made of sand and blocks
of sycamore bark, and roofed with southern
magnolia leaves. The lampposts are fashioned
from honeysuckle stems and sweetgum balls.

◖◗ Model trains traverse famous bridges and wind past
well-known landmarks.

◀ The magical scenes of the *Holiday Train Show* transport visitors to old New York with period homes such as (from left) the **Old Stone House** in Brooklyn, and Manhattan's **East 116th Street**, **Robert Livingston Beeckman House** at 854 Fifth Avenue, **Philip Kleeberg House** at 3 Riverside Drive, **17 East 128th Street**, and **167 West 23rd Street**.

17

Lighthouse (1872)
Lighthouse Park, Roosevelt Island

Legend has it that a patient at a nearby psychiatric center built this lighthouse at the tip of Roosevelt Island. An inscription reads: "This . . . work was done by John McCarthy who built the lighthouse from the bottom to the top. All ye who do pass by may pray for his soul when he dies." The replica, created in 1999, is made from sand in tinted grout with pine and hickory bark accents. The details are fashioned from pear-shaped pods, grapevine tendrils, tinted magnolia leaves, and moss.

Hendrick I. Lott House (1792)
1940 East 36th Street, Brooklyn

Still standing in the same orientation on its original site, the Lott House is a rare surviving Dutch-American house in New York City. The replica, created in 2008, has siding shingles of birch bark and pine cone scale roof shingles. Its chimneys are corkscrew hazel with cinnamon stick and twisted bark straps. The porch roof is pine bark and the foundation is oak bark. Shutters are strips of plum bark with grapevine shutter dogs and pine cone scale hinges. Porch columns are honeysuckle vines with acorn cap feet.

Ellis Island Immigration Station (1900)
New York Harbor

From 1892 to 1954, nearly 12 million people landed at Ellis Island in a quest for freedom of speech and religion, and economic opportunity. Most of those individuals were processed in the Main Building, an impressive French Renaissance structure in red brick and limestone trim, which opened in 1900 and today is the Ellis Island Immigration Museum. The stonework for the Main Building of the replica, introduced in 2007, is elm bark. The steps are sea grape leaves as are the wooden doors, which also feature gourd seeds. The window mullions are winged euonymus twigs. Corbels are gourd seeds, peppercorns, grapevine tendrils, and eucalyptus pods. The eagles have alder cone bodies with spruce cone scale wings and clove feet. The eagle perch is nuts with cloves and raffia. The towers are made of fungus, hemlock cones, spruce cones, winged euonymus branches, and several varieties of pine cone scales. The roof is made of gourds, date vines, and whole acorns.

◀ **William K. Vanderbilt Mansion** (1883)
660 Fifth Avenue, Manhattan
This limestone French Renaissance house
was said to represent a new era in residential
splendor at a time when Manhattan was
drowning in a sea of brownstone. New Yorkers
had never seen anything like the Vanderbilt
House and it was, for a time, unique on this side
of the Atlantic. It was demolished in 1926. On
the Garden's version, created in 2006, the roof
is made of eucalyptus leaves and the roof trim
of cinnamon, beechnuts, grapevine tendrils, and
alder cones. The gargoyles are magnolia pod
stems, star anise, columbine seed pods, and
alder cone scales. The porch rails on the second
and third floors are magnolia pod stems and
winged euonymus; the windows are chestnut
bark and pussy willow twigs; and the tower trim
is screwbean mesquite pods, beechnut seeds,
star anise, eucalyptus pod tops, and winged
euonymus.

◀ Olana (1891)
Hudson, New York

Olana, named for a fortress treasure-house in ancient Persia, was the home of Frederic Edwin Church, a major figure in the Hudson River School of landscape painting. Built between 1870 and 1891, it was inspired by the Moorish architecture he saw on an extended trip to Europe and the Middle East. After disengaging Richard Morris Hunt, the designer of his first house on the property, Church hired Calvert Vaux to design his new dream house. The model of Olana, introduced in 2005, has siding of horse chestnut bark and a roof of eucalyptus leaves. The ornamentation is made of pussy willow, alder cones, beech seeds and hulls, gourd seeds, winged euonymus twigs, lotus pods, star anise, and willow sticks.

◀ Lyndhurst (1865)
Tarrytown, New York
Overlooking the Hudson River in Tarrytown, this Gothic Revival-style house was designed in 1838 by Alexander Jackson Davis as a country villa for former New York City Mayor William Paulding. In 1864–65, the mansion was doubled in size for the second owner, New York merchant George Merritt. In 1961 the 67-acre estate passed from the family of the third owner, railroad tycoon Jay Gould, to the National Trust for Historic Preservation. The stonework of the replica, created in 2005, is made of elm bark. The window casings are fabricated with bamboo and salt cedar branches, while the bay window details are composed of shelf fungus, cinnamon curls, beech seeds, gourd seeds, and juniper berries.

BATTING ORDER

ICAN LEAGUE   NATIONAL LEA
TEAMS

◀ Yankee Stadium (1923)
Bronx

In 1921 the New York Yankees purchased 10 acres of property in the Bronx to build a new ballpark. The stadium, completed in just 284 days, was ready for the inaugural game on April 18, 1923, against Boston. Because legendary slugger Babe Ruth's drawing power helped make the new structure possible, it became known as "The House that Ruth Built." The classic original stadium, which underwent later redesigns and renovations and was demolished in 2010, is memorialized in the replica, created in 2005. The outside wall is made of horse chestnut bark, the seats of elm bark, and the field walls of cherry bark. The pillars are willow sticks, the light towers are willow twigs and acorn tops, and the top detailing is a combination of cinnamon sticks, winged euonymus twigs, acorn tops, and willow. LED acorn lights were added in 2009.

◀ **Enid A. Haupt Conservatory** (1902)
The New York Botanical Garden, Bronx
The Enid A. Haupt Conservatory is the
glasshouse that contains the *Holiday Train
Show* and so much more. Its design, by William
R. Cobb of the Lord & Burnham Company, was
inspired by two major glasshouses in England:
the Palm House of the Royal Botanic Gardens,
Kew, and the 1851 Crystal Palace at Hyde Park.
Conservatory architects were the first to use
curvilinear metal frames and shaped glass.
This airy structure defied the Victorian notion of
absolute solidity, at times blending into the sky.
The replica, which was created in 1998, is made
of reeds with casting resin for the glass.

◀ **Pennsylvania Station** (1910)
Eighth Avenue between 31st & 33rd Streets, Manhattan

At 20 square feet, Penn Station is the largest building replica in the *Holiday Train Show*. The original building, which spanned about eight acres, was demolished under controversy in 1964 to make way for the fourth incarnation of Madison Square Garden. The demolition is considered the catalyst for the enactment of New York City's first architectural preservation statutes. The elaborate botanical interpretation features Penn Station's Grand Concourse, set two feet above the replica's street level, and a cutaway view to the train tracks beneath the station with a shuttling passenger train. The replica, introduced in 2009, has columns made of honeysuckle; façade trim of sea grape leaves, peppercorns, viburnum, willow, and oak bark; and railings of screwbean mesquite pod, winged euonymus, willow, and acorn caps. The roof is magnolia and pine cone scales, and the skylights are winged euonymus and basket reed. The adorning eagles have white pine cone bodies, magnolia bud feathers, and acorn cap wings. The clocks are birch bark and wheat seeds, and the statues have pistachio bodies and cedrela wings.

CONEY ISLAND, BROOKLYN

◀ **Galveston Flood Building** (ca. 1906)
The Galveston Flood building once housed a
show depicting and re-creating with lighting,
mechanical, and other effects, the tidal surge
that nearly destroyed Galveston, Texas, on
September 8, 1900. It remains one of the
deadliest natural disasters in U.S. history.
People flocked to Coney Island for what was
then a multimedia extravaganza. Stars of Texas,
rendered in red twig dogwood stems, adorn each
side of the model, created in 2001.

◀ **Luna Park Arch, Central Tower, and
Ticket Booth** (1903)
Luna Park is long gone, but like many features
of Coney Island, it retains a hold on New
Yorkers' memories. Built with an Arabian theme
on 22 acres, it housed the Trip to the Moon
ride. A multitude of spires and minarets were
erected to impart a fanciful other-worldliness.
The replicas were created in 2001. The Arch is
made with gourds, eucalyptus root, and basket
jute, and hung with strands of canella berry light
bulbs. The Garden's version of the 125-foot-high
Central Tower has been fashioned from sand
in tinted grout, tree branch slices, star anise,
walnut shells, dried orange slices, rose petals,
and various seeds and gourds. The Luna Park
Ticket Booth has been re-created with cinnamon
sticks and grapevine tendrils and canella seed
pods as lights.

▶ The Jewish Museum (1909)
1109 Fifth Avenue, Manhattan
Charles Pierrepont Henry Gilbert, a prominent New York architect of
the late 19th and early 20th centuries, designed this building as a
private home for the family of Felix Warburg. Gilbert's specialty was
designing grand, chateau-style houses on Fifth Avenue for wealthy New
York patrons such as investment bankers Warburg and Otto Kahn and
entrepreneur Frank Woolworth. In 1944 the Warburg family donated
the home to The Jewish Museum, which opened in 1947. The replica,
created in 2004, has a façade of sand in tinted grout. The window
mullions and casings are made of willow, wheat stems, rose hips, and
corkscrew hazel, and the sills of maple bark. The decorative headers are
of juniper berries, acorns, and pine, hemlock, and spruce cones.
The columns are winged euonymus, acorns, spruce cones, lotus pods,
and wheat.

Foreground from left:

◀ **Eden Musée** (1883)
55 West 23rd Street, Manhattan
Destroyed in 1916 and subsequently rebuilt at Coney Island, the Eden Musée featured "the usual retinue of freaks, midgets, fire eaters, sword swallowers, waxworks, [and] a Chamber of Horrors" as Luc Sante describes so well in *Low Life*, his history of the seamy side of old New York. The model, created in 1997, has a façade of bark and roof made of oak leaves. The elaborate ornamentation is made of grapevine tendrils, nigella seed pods, dried kumquat slices, star anise, corkscrew hazel, curls of birch bark, pine cone scales, and shelf fungus.

◀ **Lycée Français de New York** (1899)
7 East 72nd Street, Manhattan
Originally the home of Oliver Gould and Mary Brewster Jennings, the curved copper and slate mansard roof, deep-set French windows, and elegant ironwork of this ornate building evoke the opulence of Napoleon III's Paris. This version, introduced in 2000, is made of sand in tinted grout, oak leaves, grapevine tendrils, pine cones, cinnamon stick slices, and dried orange slices.

◀ **Mary Mason Jones House** (1869)
Fifth Avenue at 57th Street, Manhattan
Though brownstones were the trend in New York at the time, Mary Mason Jones built a block of marble houses on the east side of Fifth Avenue between 57th and 58th Streets that became known as Marble Row. Jones, the daughter of John Mason, head of Chemical Bank, and also the great-aunt of Edith Wharton, lived in this house, which in 1929 was destroyed to make way for new construction. The façade of the replica, created in 2001, has moneta leaves cut into brick shapes with white grout and cinnamon stick edging. The roof framing is made from black eucalyptus leaves and redbud sticks, and the dormer windows and balconies are corkscrew hazel.

Background from left:

◀ **Nathan Straus House** (1896)
27 West 72nd Street, Manhattan
After Nathan Straus made his fortune as a partner of the New York department stores Abraham and Straus and R.H. Macy and Co., he turned to philanthropy. He advocated milk pasteurization as a means to check the spread of tuberculosis and provided relief for the poor during economic and natural disasters. The replica, introduced in 2003, has a stoop made of moneta leaves and willow twigs; windows adorned with cinnamon sticks, nigella pods, acorn caps, and canella berries; and a balcony made of red twig dogwood and screwbean mesquite pods.

◀ **Collectors Club** (1902)
22 East 35th Street, Manhattan
Founded in 1896, the Collectors Club is one of America's premier philatelic organizations. Its home, an elegant neo-Georgian, five-story brownstone, was completely redesigned by McKim, Mead & White in 1902. Alfred Lichtenstein, one of the giants of early philately, donated it to the Club in 1938. With columns and portals along the front, this likeness, created in 2000, is composed of broom and willow sticks, corkscrew hazel pieces, red-tinted magnolia leaves, grapevine, and acorn caps.

◀ **Thomas Fortune Ryan House** (1893)
858 Fifth Avenue, Manhattan
Transforming the ballroom into an art gallery was the largest structural change made by Thomas Fortune Ryan when he bought the house in 1905 from the original owner, dry goods merchant Isaac Stern. The house was demolished in 1939. In the model, introduced in 2006, the attic window frame is made of wheat; the top floor banding details of juniper, beech seeds, cinnamon, poppy pods, and gourd seeds; and the bay window details of shelf fungus, peppercorns, screwbean mesquite pods, radish seeds, juniper, and alder cone. The stair railing is made of wisteria seed pods.

◀ **Kykuit** (1913)
Pocantico Hills, New York
Kykuit—Dutch for "lookout"—is a 40-room villa with breathtaking
views of the Hudson River, built for oil tycoon John D. Rockefeller by the
architectural firm of Delano & Aldrich. The Classical Revival mansion's
interiors were designed by Ogden Codman, Jr. In 1979 the house, its
furnishings, and 87 of the estate's 4,000 acres were donated by his
grandson, then New York Governor Nelson Rockefeller, to the National
Trust for Historic Preservation. The replica, created in 2005, has a roof
made of magnolia leaves. The ironwork is composed of eucalyptus
leaves, stems, and seed pods; juniper berries; hickory nut shells; and
beech seed pods. Pine bark forms the stonework. The figures are
fashioned out of pistachio shells, honeysuckle vines, and wheat grain,
and their hair is made of tree lichen, yarrow, and dusty miller. The eagle
is constructed from willow leaves, ash seeds, and hickory nuts.

Grant's Tomb (1897)
122nd Street & Riverside Drive, Manhattan
Designed by John H. Duncan, the memorial is a loose copy of Mausoleus' tomb (350 B.C.)—one of the Seven Wonders of the Ancient World—in what is now southwest Turkey. It is the largest mausoleum in North America. New York City was chosen as the final resting place of Ulysses S. Grant in part so his widow, Julia, could visit daily. In 1902 she was also interred there. The mausoleum's granite and marble are represented in the replica, created in 2002, by willow, pine cones, moneta leaves, canella berries, and corkscrew hazel.

The New York Public Library (1911)
Fifth Avenue & 42nd Street, Manhattan
Considered one of the finest examples of Beaux-Arts architecture in the United States, the Library's first Director, Dr. John S. Billings, developed the basic building guidelines that were then followed by architects Carrère & Hastings. The Library's famous marble lions were named Patience and Fortitude by Mayor Fiorello LaGuardia. They were the qualities he felt New Yorkers would need to survive the Great Depression. The model, created in 2001, has stonework made of various types of bark. The central roof is magnolia leaves. The lions are made from pear-shaped pods with grapevine tendril tails, okra seed for eyes, and wild meadow grass manes.

▶ **Senator William Andrews Clark House** (1904)
Fifth Avenue & 77th Street, Manhattan
A copper king and one-term senator from Montana built this six-story,
100-plus-room Beaux-Arts mansion as a testament to his arrival in New
York. It was demolished in 1927. On the Garden's version, introduced
in 2006, the columns are made of beech sticks; the balcony supports
of palm fronds, eucalyptus buds, and acorns; the garage door awning
of yucca seed pods; and the chimneys of pistachio hulls. The adorning
ladies have okra gowns, acorn faces, lichen hair, and white peppercorn
hands. The lion has a bear paw pod face, okra seed eyes, grapevine
tendril mane, pine cone scale ears, and wheat chafe eyebrows.

◀ **Bedford Hills Station** (ca. 1870)
New York & Harlem Railroad
Bedford Hills, New York

It's just over 39 miles to Grand Central Terminal from this northern Westchester community. The replica, created in 2006, has a weather vane made of yucca and radish seeds, bamboo reed, grapevine tendrils, and juniper berries. Its steeple is mahogany pod, and its columns are winged euonymus sticks with two varieties of pine cone scales and seeds.

◀ **Philipsburg Manor** (1680)
Sleepy Hollow, New York

The Philipse family was one of the wealthiest in New York in the 18th century, and the Manor was the center of their commercial trade business. They were also among the largest slaveholders in the area and Loyalists during the Revolutionary War. As a result, the property was confiscated in 1779 and the family fled to England. Today Philipsburg Manor is a living history museum with the Manor House and a gristmill, barns, and costumed interpreters. The model, created in 1999, has elm bark for the stone walls, cattails for the upper siding, and a sycamore bark roof.

◀ **Van Cortlandt Manor** (1748)
Croton-on-Hudson, New York

Situated at the confluence of the Croton and Hudson Rivers, this stone Manor House is likely built on the foundation of an earlier fort trading post from around 1665. Pierre Van Cortlandt, New York State's first lieutenant governor, moved to the Manor with his wife in 1749, a year after it was built. The siding of the replica, created in 2005, is made of cedar bark; the chimney details are fashioned out of honeysuckle, willow, and acorn tops. Pine bark is used to make the stone, and the shutters are crafted from redbud pods. The porch posts and rails are molded from winged euonymus, and the porch floor and stairs are cedar.

From left:

◀ Boscobel (1808)
Garrison, New York

This Federal-style home overlooks Constitution Marsh on the Hudson River and sits across from the U.S. Military Academy at West Point. It was built by States Dyckman, a descendant of one of the early Dutch families of New Amsterdam. On the replica, which was created in 1999, the columns are made of willow branches with acorn caps and pine cone scales. The windows, mullions, and casings are of honeysuckle twigs; the dentil moldings are cross sections of cinnamon curls; the rails are corkscrew hazel with grapevine tendrils and acorn caps atop the roof rails. The door wreath includes pine cone scales and whole hemlock cones.

◀ King Manor (1730)
Jamaica Avenue, Queens

Rufus King was an important figure in early U.S. history and a lifelong opponent of slavery. A delegate to the Constitutional Convention in 1787, he then became a New York Senator. He was also ambassador to Great Britain and ran for President against James Monroe in 1816. King purchased the 11 acres of land and its buildings, including the oldest house in Jamaica, Queens, for $12,000 in 1805. After his death the estate went to his son, John Alsop King, who became Governor of New York. The walls of the replica, which was created in 1992, are made of white birch bark, the shutters of redbud seed pods, and the roof of wheat.

▶ **St. Patrick's Cathedral** (1879)
Fifth Avenue between 50th & 51st Streets, Manhattan
A glorious structure by James Renwick, Jr., and William Rodrigue, St. Patrick's is the largest Gothic-style Roman Catholic cathedral in the United States. The Catholic Church bought the land in 1828 intending to use it as a cemetery, but abandoned the plan when gravediggers hit rock just below the surface. Intricately carved granite is cleverly replicated with dozens of different plants, including eucalyptus leaves and pods, pepper berries, Siberian iris seed pods, and gourds. The replica was added to the *Holiday Train Show* in 2003 and organ music in 2009.

◀ City Hall (1812)
City Hall Park between Broadway & Park Row, Manhattan
The design for City Hall was conceived of as a grand combination of
Federal style with French Renaissance detail by Joseph François Mangin,
a French architect who worked on Place de la Concorde in Paris, and
John McComb, Jr., a well-known New York City architect. Its original
façade, fabricated with soft Massachusetts marble, eroded badly and
was replaced with Alabama limestone. The replica, created in 2003,
is fashioned from hickory, elm, and maple bark with Virginia creeper,
honeysuckle twigs, pine cone scales, dusty miller leaves, okra seeds,
acorn tops, and corkscrew hazel. The statue of Justice is made with palm
and tobacco leaves, cattail stems, raffia, wheat, and butternut hickory.
The flagpoles are formed from red twig dogwood with bittersweet vines,
acorns, and honey locust pods.

CENTRAL PARK, MANHATTAN

● Belvedere Castle (1872)

Designed by Frederick Law Olmsted and Calvert Vaux as a Victorian "folly," Belvedere Castle includes Gothic, Romanesque, Chinese, Moorish, and Egyptian motifs. At the highest natural elevation in the Park, the Belvedere—Italian for "beautiful view"—offers visitors just that. The front façade of the model, created in 2002, is brown-dyed flax grass with bark "brickwork." The turrets are made from pear-shaped pods, grapevine, and corkscrew hazel trimming with roof shingles of eucalyptus.

● Gothic Arch, Bridge No. 28 (1861)

Designed by Calvert Vaux and Jacob Wrey Mould, this wonderful Gothic Revival bridge was made of cast iron and steel by Cornell Iron Works. The ubiquity of horses throughout the city when it was built influenced its design and the creation of trails throughout the Park, which were deliberately created with curves to discourage horse racing. The bridge replica, created in 2002, is fashioned of corkscrew hazel, cinnamon slices, canella berries, grass fiber rope, and acorn caps.

Other Central Park structures in the *Holiday Train Show* collection include Angel of the Waters atop Bethesda Fountain, the Dairy, the Music Pavilion, and Cop Cot.

▶ Manhattan Bridge (1909)

Like the Brooklyn and Williamsburg Bridges, the Manhattan Bridge also spans the East River. Its impressive entryway on the Manhattan side was designed by the architectural firm Carrère and Hastings. The replica, created in 2002, is made of oak, hickory, and elm bark, and willow branches.

John Peden

◣ Solomon R. Guggenheim Museum (1959)
1071 Fifth Avenue, Manhattan
Frank Lloyd Wright's only design in New York City, the Guggenheim
Museum is one of the city's most unique and controversial buildings. A
symphony of triangles, ovals, arcs, circles, and squares, its central spiral
form recalls a nautilus shell with continuous spaces flowing freely into
one another. The modern and contemporary art is displayed on the walls
of a ramp in the center of the spiral that gradually rises to 92 feet, with
galleries extending off of it. The replica, introduced in 2001, is fabricated
from black locust shelf fungus.

◀ Statue of Liberty (1886)
Liberty Island, New York Harbor
A gift from the French to commemorate the centennial of the Declaration
of Independence, the statue was designed by Fréderic-Auguste Bartholdi
and shipped to America in 350 pieces. The pedestal, designed by
Richard Morris Hunt, was paid for with private donations. From the
ground to the tip of her torch, the statue measures 305 feet. The robes
of the Garden's Lady Liberty, introduced in 2001, are made from palm
fronds and grasses, her necklace from stalks of wheat, and her torch
flame from a dried monarch flower inside a pomegranate half.

Part of the fun in viewing the *Holiday Train Show*
is exploring the intricate details of each replica
and trying to identify the plant parts used for
every architectural element.

From left:

◀ **Strang-Durrin House** (18th century)
Peekskill, New York
The roof is made of eucalyptus leaves. The
window mullions are honeysuckle and the
window casings willow twigs. The replica was
created in 1999.

◀ **Guyon-Lake-Tysen House** (1740)
Richmond Road, Staten Island
The roof is made of pine bark shingles and the
chimneys of a variety of branches, including
winged euonymus. The siding is turkey-tail
fungus, the porch posts grapevines, and the
vines grapevine tendrils with rice grass and
canella berries. The replica was created in 1992
for the first train show.

◀ **Bedford Hills Station** (see page 45)

THE COLLECTION

Each year the *Holiday Train Show* is enlivened by a new design featuring different settings and landmarks from the Botanical Garden's collection of more than 140 structures. Red entries are pictured in this book.

BRONX

- Bartow-Pell Mansion (1836–1842)
  Pelham Bay Park
- Engine Company 43/
  Ladder Company 59 (1920)
  1901 Sedgwick Avenue

The New York Botanical Garden

- Great Garden Clock (1997)
- Enid A. Haupt Conservatory (1902)
- Lillian and Amy Goldman Stone
  Mill (1840)
- Poe Cottage (ca. 1812)
  Grand Concourse
- Riverdale, Spuyten Duyvil,
  Kingsbridge Memorial Bell Tower
  (1930)
  Bell Tower Park
- Squad Company 41 (ca. 1904)
  330 East 150th Street
- Valentine-Varian House (1758)
  3266 Bainbridge Avenue
- Van Cortlandt House (1749)
  Van Cortlandt Park
- Wave Hill House (1844)
  (originally William Lewis Morris
  House)
- Yankee Stadium (1923)
  (demolished 2010)

BROOKLYN

Coney Island

- Galveston Flood Building (ca. 1906)
- Luna Park Arch, Central Tower, and
  Ticket Booth (1903)
- Lefferts Homestead (1783)
  Prospect Park
- Hendrick I. Lott House (1792)
  1940 East 36th Street
- James L. Morgan House (1870)
  7 Pierrepont Street
- Old Stone House (1699)
  J.J. Byrne Park
  Fifth Avenue at Third Street

- Row House, brownstone (ca. 1860)
  Washington Park
- Williamsburg Art and Historical
  Society (1868)
  (originally King's County Savings
  Bank)
  135 Broadway at Bedford Avenue
- Pieter Claesen Wyckoff House (1652)
  5902 Clarendon Road

MANHATTAN

- Aguilar Library (1899)
  174 East 110th Street
- Apartment Building (ca. 1880)
- Apollo Theater (1914)
  253 West 125th Street
- Charles Ward Apthorpe Mansion
  (1764)
  91st Street & Columbus Avenue
  (demolished 1892)
- Robert Livingston Beeckman House
  (1905)
  854 Fifth Avenue
- Mrs. George T. Bliss House (1907)
  9 East 68th Street
- Brooks Brothers (1915)
  346 Madison Avenue
- David S. Brown Store (1876)
  8 Thomas Street

Central Park

- Angel of the Waters, Bethesda
  Fountain (1873)
- Belvedere Castle (1872)
- Cop Cot (ca. 1860)
- The Dairy (1870)
- Gazebo (1860)
- Gothic Arch, Bridge No. 28 (1861)
- Music Pavilion (1862)
- Swedish Cottage Marionette
  Theater (1876)
- Chrysler Building (1930)
  405 Lexington Avenue
- City Hall (1812)
  City Hall Park between Broadway &
  Park Row

- Senator William Andrews Clark
  House (1904)
  Fifth Avenue & 77th Street
  (demolished 1927)
- Collectors Club (1902)
  (originally Thomas B. Clarke House)
  22 East 35th Street

Commercial Buildings

- 167 West 23rd Street (1898)
- 169 West 23rd Street (1898)
- 171 Duane Street (ca. 1859)
- 93 Reade Street (1857)
- Converted Carriage House (1909)
  124 East 19th Street
- Dyckman House (1785)
  4881 Broadway & West 204th Street
- Eden Musée (1883)
  55 West 23rd Street
- Empire State Building (1931)
  350 Fifth Avenue
- Estonian House (1899)
  (originally Civic Club)
  243 East 34th Street
- Edith and Ernesto G. Fabbri House
  (1900)
  11 East 62nd Street
- Flatiron Building (1903)
  (originally Fuller Building)
  175 Fifth Avenue
- Folies Bergère Theater (1911)
  210 West 46th Street
- Frick Collection (1914)
  (originally Henry Clay Frick House)
  1 East 70th Street
- Gracie Mansion (1804)
  (originally Archibald Gracie House)
  Carl Schurz Park
- Grand Central Terminal (1913)
  42nd Street & Park Avenue
- Grant's Tomb (1897)
  General Grant National Memorial
  122nd Street & Riverside Drive
- Solomon R. Guggenheim Museum
  (1959)
  1071 Fifth Avenue

- High Bridge Water Tower (1872)
  Highbridge Park at West 173rd Street
- The Jewish Museum (1909)
  (originally Felix Warburg House)
  1109 Fifth Avenue
- Mary Mason Jones House (1869)
  Fifth Avenue at 57th Street
  (demolished 1929)
- Philip Kleeberg House (1898)
  3 Riverside Drive
- J.F.D. Lanier House (1903)
  123 East 35th Street
- Liederkranz Club (1904)
  (originally Phipps House)
  6 East 87th Street
- Lycée Français de New York (1899)
  (originally Oliver Gould Jennings
  House)
  7 East 72nd Street
- Manhattan Country School (1913)
  (originally Ogden Codman, Jr. House)
  7 East 96th Street
- Merchant's House Museum (1832)
  (originally Seabury Tredwell House)
  29 East Fourth Street
- Metropolitan Life Insurance Company
  (1909)
  1 Madison Avenue
- The Metropolitan Museum of Art
  (1880–1911)
  1000 Fifth Avenue
- Morris-Jumel Mansion (1765)
  (originally Roger and Mary Phillipse
  House)
  Jumel Terrace
- Jordan L. Mott House (1880)
  2122 Fifth Avenue
  (demolished 1936)
- Municipal Building (1914)
  1 Centre Street
- National Arts Club (1884)
  (originally Samuel J. Tilden House)
  15 Gramercy Park South
- New Amsterdam Theater (1903)
  214 West 42nd Street

- New India House (1903)
(originally Marshall Orme Wilson House)
3 East 64th Street
- The New York Public Library (1911)
Fifth Avenue & 42nd Street
- New York Stock Exchange (1903)
18 Broad Street
- Pennsylvania Station (1910)
Eighth Avenue between 31st
& 33rd Streets
(demolished 1964)
- The Plaza Hotel (1907)
Fifth Avenue at Central Park South
- Public Baths, City of New York (1906)
East 23rd Street & Asser Levy Place
- Queens Insurance Company (1877)
37 & 39 Wall Street

Rockefeller Plaza
- Channel Gardens, Holiday Tree, and Skating Rink (1932–1940)
- Radio City Music Hall (1932)
- General Electric Building (1933)
(originally RCA Building)
- Prometheus (1934)
- Theodore Roosevelt Birthplace (1848)
28 East 20th Street
- Rose Center for Earth and Space (2000)
The American Museum of Natural History
Central Park West at 81st Street

Row Houses
- 153 Bleecker Street (1830)
- East 116th Street
- 17 East 128th Street (1864)
- 28 West 54th Street (1881)
- Brownstone (ca. 1881)
West 54th Street
- Address unknown (ca. 1880)
- Address unknown (ca. 1885)
- Address unknown (ca. 1890)
- Thomas Fortune Ryan House (1893)
(originally Isaac Stern House)
858 Fifth Avenue
(demolished 1939)

- Saks Fifth Avenue (1924)
611 Fifth Avenue
- Scheffel Hall (1894)
190 Third Avenue
- Mrs. Josephine Schmid House (1895)
Fifth Avenue & 62nd Street
- Schumann's Sons (1909)
716 Fifth Avenue

South Street Seaport Historic District (ca. 1793–1811)
- 91 South Street
- Corner of Fulton and South Streets
- Schermerhorn Row, 4 Fulton Street
- Church of St. Nicholas (1914)
155 Cedar Street
- St. Patrick's Cathedral (1879)
Fifth Avenue between 50th & 51st Streets
- Willard Straight House (1915)
1130 Fifth Avenue
- Nathan Straus House (1896)
27 West 72nd Street
- Tammany Hall (1868)
14th Street
- Samuel Trowbridge House (1903)
123 East 70th Street
- United Nations Headquarters (1947–1953)
United Nations Plaza
- William K. Vanderbilt Mansion (1883)
660 Fifth Avenue
(demolished 1926)
- Claude A. Vissani House (1889)
143 West 95th Street
- Washington Arch (1895)
Washington Square Park

QUEENS
- Bowne House (1661)
37-01 Bowne Street
- Hell Gate Bridge (1917)
East River Arch Bridge of the New York Connecting Railroad
- King Manor (1730)
Jamaica Avenue

- Kingsland Homestead (1785)
143-35 37th Avenue
- Queens County Farm (1772)
(originally Jacob Adriance Farmhouse)
73-50 Little Neck Parkway
- Trans World Airlines Flight Center (1962)
John F. Kennedy International Airport

STATEN ISLAND
- Alice Austen House (mid-19th century)
2 Hylan Boulevard
- Conference House (1680)
(originally Capt. Christopher Billopp House)
Hylan Boulevard
- Guyon-Lake-Tysen House (1740)
Richmondtown Restoration
Richmond Road
- Joseph H. Seguine House (1837)
440 Seguine Avenue

BRIDGES AND ISLANDS OF NEW YORK CITY
- Brooklyn Bridge (1883)
- Ellis Island Immigration Station (1900)
New York Harbor
- George Washington Bridge (1931)
- High Bridge (Aqueduct Bridge) (1848)
Highbridge Park at West 174th Street
- Lighthouse (1872)
Lighthouse Park
Roosevelt Island
- Little Red Lighthouse (1880)
Below the George Washington Bridge
- Manhattan Bridge (1909)
- Statue of Liberty (1886)
Liberty Island, New York Harbor

NEW YORK'S HUDSON RIVER VALLEY AND BEYOND
- Bedford Hills Station (ca. 1870)
New York & Harlem Railroad
Bedford Hills
- Boscobel (1808)
Garrison

- Highland Gardens (1838)
Newburgh
- Hurst-Pierrepont Estate (1867)
Garrison
- Kykuit (1913)
Rockefeller Estate
Pocantico Hills
- Lyndhurst (1865)
Tarrytown
- Montgomery Place (1805)
Annandale-on-Hudson
- Olana (1891)
Frederic Edwin Church Residence
Hudson
- Philipsburg Manor (1680)
Sleepy Hollow
- Strang-Durrin House (18th century)
Peekskill
- Sunnyside (1835)
Washington Irving Residence
Tarrytown
- Van Cortlandt Manor (1748)
Croton-on-Hudson

Editors
Carol Capobianco
Karen Daubmann
Margaret Falk
Sally Armstrong Leone
Jean Mayfield-Morelli

Designer
Susan Siegrist

Creative Direction
Terry Skoda

Principal Photographer
Robert Benson

© 2010
The New York Botanical Garden

ISBN 978-0-89327-973-8

John Peden

About Paul Busse

What one may see as just a piece of bark or a fallen berry, *Holiday Train Show* creator Paul Busse envisions as stone on the Brooklyn Bridge or an ornament on St. Patrick's Cathedral. On a walk through the woods on his property in Alexandria, Kentucky, where he and his wife, Margaret, and son, Brian, run their design company Applied Imagination, he and the artists on his team inevitably bring back some interesting tidbit that can be used in crafting one of his magical displays.

His story could have been different if he didn't take the path—or track—less traveled. After earning a landscape architecture degree from Ohio State University in 1972, Paul expected to go the conventional route and land a steady job somewhere. But he realized during a job interview that that type of lifestyle wasn't for him.

"If I had continued as a landscape architect, if I'd done more routine stuff, I probably could have made more money and had a big nursery by now. But that never interested me," Paul told *Kentucky Living* magazine in 2006. "I don't just want to run a business. Whenever it came to a choice in life, I've always taken the more creative option."

This thinking led Paul to his own business in garden railway design in 1982, when he created his first model exhibition for the Ohio State Fair. Ten years later, his reputation as a designer of wondrous landscapes built around trains and structures made from plant parts took off when he mounted the first *Holiday Train Show* for The New York Botanical Garden.

Since then, he has produced special exhibits for many other venues around the country, including the U.S. Botanic Garden, the Chicago Botanic Garden, Longwood Gardens, and the Morris Arboretum. A documentary about Paul and his work, *Holiday Train Show with David Hartman*, airs on PBS stations around the holidays. Current work can be viewed at appliedimagination.biz